praise for shee

Shee writes with wisdom, honesty, and empathy that is totally unique to her. *If You Cannot Find Her* is a beautiful reminder that life is a gift that also brings much heartache - but within the heartache, we can find many lessons that will mold us into the person we were meant to be. It is a gorgeous, incomparable debut book - one that needs to be read.

CHLOÉ MARIA WINSTANLEY,
AUTHOR OF *FEMINITICH: POEMS FOR THE MODERN WITCH*

if you cannot find her

if you cannot find her

A COLLECTION OF POETRY & PROSE

SHEE

I feel, therefore I am.

BERLIOZ

Copyright © 2019 by Shee

All rights reserved.

No part of this book may be reproduced in any form or by any electronic or mechanical means, including information storage and retrieval systems, without written permission from the author, except for the use of brief quotations in a book review.

Cover layout design by: Shee

Book format design by: Shee Edited by: Chloé Maria Winstanley Cover art: www.pexels.com

Irina Iriser

@iriser_k

ISBN: **978-1-7340199-2-6**

Imprint: Independently published

For information regarding permission or distribution, contact Shee. poetry@gmail.com for contact and other information, including upcoming releases, promotions, and events.

For my Forever Family Andres, Jacob, Messiah, Aiden, & May

foreword

They want me to talk about love and sunshine. The way the light kisses the hills. The way the ocean plays tag with the shore. They want me to dish on romance and tell of my favorite bubble gum lollipops. Only the light will do for them. Do not show them one ounce of darkness, or they shall turn their back on everything you are doing your best to reveal, but this isn't about them. This is the way out of obscurity for many. This is about the climb from a pit of pain no sugar-coat can sweeten. This is sadness in all of its sour, unveiled for anyone who cares to read. This is it, and I won't change. This is me, formed in poetry.

-Shee, 2019

A Message to the Reader:
First, I'd like to say thank you for choosing to pick up this book out of the hundreds of thousands of beautiful poetry books that are in circulation today. It is still mind-boggling to me that there are people who enjoy my work and can connect on different levels. For a long time, I had no idea if I would be able to pull this off and kept postponing it. Please know that I am not a trendy writer, and I don't follow a lot of standard poetry practices; I write what feels right.

One of the reasons it has taken me so long to put this collection out there is insecurity. Are my words good enough? I still struggle with these notions, and although I'm sure I will have people who won't enjoy my work, this is one of my biggest goals in life, and I don't want to regret not going through with it. So, here we are.

Another reason is, self-publishing is not for the faint of heart. It takes a lot of work and motivation to be able to put a manuscript together (even a collection of poetry) and, it does not mean you will be successful. However, I am a firm believer in everything happening for a reason, and that this book will reach who it needs to and when it does, it will be home. Even if for a little while.

I've sat down several times and attempted to write this letter to you all. How can I put into words how grateful I am for the opportunity to share these pieces of me with you? Honestly, I can't. There are no words that can express how thankful I am for all of this. It is surreal even writing this bit.

Like many poets, I've been writing on and off for most of my life. This outlet has saved me from me on my worst days, and I believe it can do the same for everyone out there. I encourage you all to give writing a try. How you decide to pen, does not have to make sense to anyone other than you. No pressure, but, give it a try and see how wonderful it feels to get things off of your chest and onto paper, your phone, napkins...wherever you see fit.

Before you dive into the book, I want to let you know what you can expect. There is no dominant theme to this collection, other than heartbreak and several pieces about the Moon, which I didn't intend, although, I won't apologize because I adore the Moon. However, it just so happens that most of these pieces reflect upon the years they were written. This collection is evidence of a journey within a journey. This collection is like a homecoming, an album, proof that I existed. Pieces of my history that I was ashamed of for so long, but not anymore.

You will notice that some parts are interactive, asking you to fill in blanks. I don't want you to only write in those spaces but all over the book; write notes, your poems, your disagreements with what you may read, whatever. Let this book become a journal that you can refer back to when you're living in similar situations. Also, as a disclaimer, you will find pieces that may trigger you, and although I do not want to offend or hurt anyone, this collection shares some sensitive content related to sexual abuse, suicide attempt, and mental health.

I am an emotional creature who can never live a moment once. When I write about the past, it is as if I am reliving that situation once again. There are days I am free from pain, "forgiveness in tow," and then there are the days where I can barely breathe from it all. My mind is continually battling my heart; both (body and soul) having their own opinion on my life and circumstance. Be it as it may... the words flow from both. Maybe what I am asking is that you find an appreciation (or an understanding) for the apparent contradiction from piece to piece.

I promise you, happiness lives here too, but you may

INTRODUCTION

find it hard to find optimism within these pages. As the title of this book may hint when I wrote the majority of these pieces, I was lost; looking for a way to be. The only way I was able to find my way out of the fog was through words. I am forever grateful for finding my voice, something I will never take for granted. I hope that someone out there will be encouraged by my words enough to find their voice.

Although most of what I write is from personal experience, a lot of what I write is from people watching and observation. I hope I'm able to do those stories justice; anything I have witnessed and felt in my heart is etched within the folds of my soul. Much of what you read may be construed as romantic heartbreak, some yes, but not all. I hope that when you read, you will interpret the poems as they fit in your life. Some poems will not affect you, or maybe you will not be able to relate. That is perfectly fine. Perhaps it will never connect, but you will possibly know someone who needs to read it, and you will share.

So, to you, my beloved reader, thank you. Thank you for holding pieces of my heart within your hands and showing the world that intimacy can be as simple as reading a stranger's poem. If there is anything, I hope you can learn from this collection it is that growth, courage, and love come in different degrees, times, shades of color, possibilities, and depth.

If who you love is proof of who we are as humans, then damn, I must be amazing. I love you all.

-Shee, 2019

I do not intend to lose people
They slip away before I know to reach out my fingers
As a reminder that I'm still here
Don't leave me
I'm still here
Should I have to remind people that I still exist?
Maybe?
I don't know the answer
Or perhaps, I do
But it hurts more to admit
That I'm not worth holding on to
That it is too much trouble
Loving a broken soul
I'm so bad at the knowing

I'm getting used to
Losing the relationships where
I did most of the tending
I don't want to
I don't want to be used to disappointment and loss
I don't want to know that
Regardless of how much I love another
They'll leave anyway
That one day I will feel like
The weight of the world
Is about to crush me
And there won't be anyone there
To help me out of the rubble
But I know
I'm so good at the knowing

SHEE

And if I had to choose
Between the day or night
I would choose the night
Once
And then again
And again
Because somehow these words
Get lost in the light
And it is only the Moon
That can help me find them again

IF YOU CANNOT FIND HER

You are beautiful,
You are beautiful because you are kind.
Kind, in a world that tells you,
There is no value in being you.

You are beautiful because you relay sweet messages,
To petal-less flowers to motivate them to grow.
You sing to the dark side of the Moon,
Knowing he is in love with the Sun.

You walk barefoot through grass,
To communicate with the Earth.
You meditate in deep waters,
To acknowledge its healing.

You love hard,
So, no one who comes to know you,
Will have to feel rejection like you have.
Everything you do is to balance out the negative,
To push out nothing but positivity so evil won't prevail.

Too selfless to ever be selfish.
You are beautiful!
So.
Damn.
Beautiful.

You are beautiful because you are…

You.

SHEE

Create roots!!! **They say**
Like the trees in the forest.
You'll live forever!

I can do no such thing
See, the trees are beautiful and robust
Tireless in their ambition
Working in unison
As the heartbeat of the forest
But I could never be a tree

I'd much rather be the wind

Yes, the wind…
Free to move as fast and fierce as I choose
Flying between the heavens and Earth
Belonging only to the rhythm of life
Choreographing the dances of the ocean
Allowing itself to be wild with freedom
Telling secrets to anyone who will listen

I'd much rather be the wind

IF YOU CANNOT FIND HER

When you miss me
Let the Sun kiss your skin
I will always be with you
Always

To my loves

SHEE

Have you ever been lost in circles?
Picking up the fallen pieces of your broken heart?
Wondering what you did wrong to deserve limited love?

Let me chip at that circle and bring you home
How others have loved you
Is not a reflection of the love you deserve

Honey, love is not a shape
It is a road, lined with blooming flowers
Feeding off the goodness of the Sun

Let's take a walk
And I'll show you what you've been missing
I'll show you a seed of love
You can grow on your own

Self-Love

IF YOU CANNOT FIND HER

Who would've guessed
That I would learn to love myself
Before you ever could

I learned in the waiting…

SHEE

I feel it on the days where I can't stay warm
On the days where my mind wanders from reality
And, when my legs feel weak
And won't comply with gravity
Those days…
Those days are when I feel it most

Abandoned

IF YOU CANNOT FIND HER

She's never been that girl
The one who the other girls call
When they want to party
Or just hang

No, she's never been her
She's always been the girl
Who brings you cozy blankets
Who serves you warm cups of tea
Who wipes away your tears
All without expecting anything in return

She's the girl who puts out fires
Fires ignited by those who
Had no intention of ever turning them off

She's the girl you call to clean up messes
Messes of a broken heart
And, she's okay with that

She will always be who you need her to be
Even if you can't be that for her

She's that girl

SHEE

Move on...
They say it like it's a choice they can make for me
Move on?! Okay.
So, I move closer to the line of fire
Because Mama didn't raise a quitter
Even if she did raise a fool

Fool for Love

IF YOU CANNOT FIND HER

Isn't it obvious?
That everything I have done
Everything I continue to do
Is to save the world?

To save those who drown by air?
To rescue those who swim through thorns?
To resuscitate those who have swallowed glass?

Maybe I want to be the hero
Or maybe I have no choice
I shall save anyone who dares need me
Anyone who speaks my name
Those who choose not to breathe
The ones who do not smell the flowers
The souls who have no appreciation of wine

Because to me, it is obvious
It is me who needs saving
Even if I wear an invisible cape

Who will stop to teach me lessons in being?
Who will show me how to appreciate the blossoms?
Who will give me a chance to sip God's red nectar?

No amount of cape can ever hide who I've always been
A woman stuck in hope as thick as mud
I keep saving in hopes of being saved
I keep teaching in hopes of being taught
I keep loving in hopes of being loved

Isn't it obvious?

SHEE

They tell me I am nothing
But blood and bones
But they are wrong

I am more
I am, if nothing else
A creation of stardust and Moon rocks

For my whole life is built upon wishes to fallen stars
And serenades to a lonely Moon

Oh, how I love to sing to the Moon

IF YOU CANNOT FIND HER

Forgiveness is a mask
A mask we wear to make others feel better

A mask we wear to allow others
To move on after they've hurt us

We do not forgive
We do not know how
We simply allow

We allow the pain to be okay
We allow betrayal to go to sleep
We allow our heart to continue to beat

We are not capable of forgiveness
Because we cannot forget

But our skin becomes tougher
Our eyes become brighter
And our laughs become hopeful

We do what we must to move on
Because some things are not worth the burden

Some things are not worth our peace

If I was given a choice
Between lightning and thunder
I'd choose thunder
Because as much as I'd like to be seen
I'd much rather be heard

IF YOU CANNOT FIND HER

You tell me I've changed
Like you want to offend me
The only insult is that you believe
You weren't the reason behind the evolving

SHEE

I loved you before I ever loved myself
Expecting you to teach me how
It was only in the ways you did not love me
Where I learned I could
Love me all on my own

All on my own

IF YOU CANNOT FIND HER

I whispered my prayer for you
Onto the wings of a butterfly
Did you get it?

You are loved...

SHEE

I slip back into you
Like you're made of silk and lace
But become entangled in your web of loathing

I tirelessly remind myself
That you are more thorn than rose
All prickly but an easy distraction

It doesn't matter that you are ice disguised as flame
Because I am little more
Than trembling hands
Looking for warmth

DEPRESSION

IF YOU CANNOT FIND HER

And,
if you love her
you will let her bloom
but on her own
and on her own time

I hide behind paper and pen
Because words have been kinder to me
More than people ever have

IF YOU CANNOT FIND HER

You only desire to touch me
When I am soft and free of thorns
Most days I am tough and rigid
Too aggressive for you to hold

I do not do easy
Nor has easy ever done me
It is never when I am delicate
When I need your fingers to trace
Across my surface with affection

It is always when I am hardened from the world
That I need the touch of kind words
To help me thrive again

It kept her alive
But killed her inside
Her nemesis
Her heart

I want to love, Love
    Like the Sun wants to rise
    And the Moon wants to shine
    Like a flower wants to bloom
    And the wind wants to blow

I want to love, Love
    Even when the Sun cannot be warmth
    Or when the Moon seeks to hide
    Even when a flower loses her petals
    Or when the wind needs its rest

I will love, Love.
    In all ways
    Always

SHEE

All I've wanted
More times than not
Was to stop loving you
To stop believing
That the Sun rose
Because you breathe

But what all the wishing
Has shown me
Is that my heart
Is not a quitter
Even if yours
Quit me so long ago

IF YOU CANNOT FIND HER

If you see Sadness in my eyes
Please do not attempt to remove what clearly belongs

The Moon, with all its grandeur and genius
Already tried to lift away the weary ghosts
Who have found solace behind these lids, to no avail

So, I sit back and wait longingly for the days
That Sadness will become filled with boredom
It will leave to play in the rain

But we all know the Sun will come back to glitter the sky
And Sadness will race its way back again
To my dark brown eyes
Because only darkness will do

If you see Sadness in my eyes
Know Sadness doesn't live here
It comes and goes as it pleases
And, I haven't the heart to keep these eyes closed

Because even Sadness needs
A place to rest its weary head

Sadness needs love too

He was chaos wrapped in beauty

All the heartbreakers are

IF YOU CANNOT FIND HER

It's not raining today
But I wore my rain boots anyway

I want to sing in the rain
Dance in hopeful puddles
And laugh as droplets kiss my nose

It's not raining today
But I wore my rain boots anyway

Wishful thinking

SHEE

They stare at me
Waiting for me to give them
What they so freely give me

But I'm numb and broken
Lost and distracted in distorted emotion
Unable to feel the Sunshine
That once kept me warm with joy

And maybe I have no excuse
Or maybe I have a million
Even if it seems unreachable
I push myself to be who they need me to be

So, even on the coldest days I chase happiness
Just for a taste, even a touch

I don't want to hold it captive
No, he can come and go as he pleases
Because I just want to be his friend
To lean on him when my days are dark
Or, when laughter is missing from my belly
Especially on the days when little hands need to play

See, I'm not greedy
Not even close
But I have three little beating hearts
Who I need more than they need me

So, I keep chasing hoping one day Happiness
Will slow down and, share his life with me

For Marlette

IF YOU CANNOT FIND HER

It isn't easy
This being left behind

SHEE

The truth is, I miss you
Bonded through blood
Separated by differences

Confusion and regret
Lie within the folds of my heart
Heartbreak extends to the tips of these fingers

Rejection never easy to swallow
So, I will wait between
What used to be
And what will never be

Because that is where we left off
And the fact will remain
I have no choice but to miss you

Sometimes I whisper my woes into the wind
For the pain is too heavy for one soul to hold
So, I whisper and let the wind do what it does best

LEAVE

I know you hear the wind whispering my name…
I hope it hurts

SHEE

You told me you dream of oceans
Something you have never seen

Me?
I dream of people who have never loved me
But love me in my sleep

We both have things we have never experienced
But dream they may come true

Yours may one day become reality
Whereas mine will only stay a dream

As dramatic as it may sound
I feel everything

The roll of your eyes
When I tell you I'm hurting

The heavy sigh
As I crumble into emotion

The angry beat of your heart
When I say too much

The furrow of your brow
When I'm weak from pain

Not only was I born into a life
Of unfortunate circumstances

But I have been forced to feel
The disappointment of others

Who choose to break away from understanding

Those who forget compassion
Is as simple as a listening ear

I. FEEL. EVERYTHING.

SHEE

She knew it was going to burn
She touched it anyway
Love

               How brave she is

She is…
>A beautiful mess of contradiction
>With just enough sparkle to accent her darkness
>Just enough giggle to accompany her cry

She was more of what this world needed
>But less than what was appreciated
>She was what was right in the world
>But even she could not believe it

SHEE

She always fell heart first
    It was her nature
    It was the strongest part of her
    Until, it was not

Eventually her heart became her weakness
    Cracked and fragile from years of pain
    But that's what makes for the best stories
    And, she always loved a good book

Give her a good ending, please

IF YOU CANNOT FIND HER

_____
_____
_____
_____
_____
_____
_____
_____

…happens when you have an irresponsible heart…

BOOK

God, you're beautiful
He would whisper with hot breath in my ear
Never had I wished more for God
To take away my hearing
Like I did those years

But it would have done nothing
Because the words would have still crawled up my ear
Into my throat, choking me into silent tears
Maybe as he touched me
In the place Mama called my ***book***
He was thinking of another
Or did a once happy little girl
Give him the pleasure most men seek
From full breasts and curved hips

Ay, Anak, close your book
My mother's voice would say in my head
As he burned his fingers into my soul
Why me?
Mama, why me?!

I kept my book closed
Yet he opened it ruthlessly
Like he owned the words
That would eventually flow
From the pain he enforced upon it

Mama!
Mama, I'm sorry, I tried.

IF YOU CANNOT FIND HER

I don't care!
Lie to me!
I need something to keep going.
Tell me again, please!

The stars shine, just for you.

You're the type of person
To start a fire
And blame the match

Name of Fire Starter

IF YOU CANNOT FIND HER

She always wondered
Where those butterflies had gone
She wanted them back
She missed the tickle of new love

MAYBE

To be blessed is to watch
The way my husband fathers my daughter
And, the way my little girl daughters her father
Their relationship, their bond
The stuff of magic, I swear
I observe every pinky promise
The giggles and inside jokes
The finger pointing when Mommy is the bad guy
The Thursday surprises when he comes home from work
The way their noses bunch up in unison, like twins
When they smell something yucky
Their identical feet, that hate wearing socks
The hypnotizing honey color of their eyes, reminding me
I've never seen anything as sweet
The way my husband admires her with pride in his eyes
As she twirls around in her new dress she just had to have
And, as much as my heart smiles, it also aches a bit
Because the love they share, I've never known
And, although I may share a face like his
My father has never been mine
For years I thought I would never be able to fill that void
But the universe has a way of listening
And making up for its mistakes
Because anything I've ever wished for and never received
The Universe has given to her
And maybe, that's enough for me
Even if I was never enough for him

Sometimes, happily ever after
  Begins with a broken heart

Even if the pain was crippling
Maybe I wanted the heartbreak
So I had something to write about

Let's call it inspiration...

I touch the wound
A little push to see if it's still tender
I wince as it awakens
Still there

I shall check again when it seems to have scabbed over

Like a security blanket, I fear for its absence
I don't want it to leave

But I am too grown to hold onto
Tattered pieces of what once was

What does this say of me?

I'm terrible at healing

I am distracted by all of this pain
The pain is not mine
But I will bear it for you
Give it to me
I will make it mine

I wonder if the old you misses me too…

I miss (who) you (were).

SHEE

I am the last few pages of an unfinished book
A loose penny not worth the effort to spend
The last drops of ink in a thrown away pen
The ash and embers of a once roaring fire
A scrap of silk from a Queen's ball gown

See I am most times forgotten
Overlooked and dismissed
But I am more
So much more

I am the dew drops on a lonely flower
A cool breeze on a hot Summer day
The fizzy bubbles atop a root beer float
A deep breath after a romantic kiss
Cotton candy skies as the Sun heads to bed

I. Am.

IF YOU CANNOT FIND HER

It hurts, but it still beats.

SHEE

Happiness pirouettes
Atop the fluttering wings
Of a hummingbird
Teasing me
Dancing merrily
In my line of sight

Never close enough for me to catch it
But only long enough
For me to admire
Its impeccably choreographed routine

For, if I did
I wouldn't have the heart
To let it free
And would only allow it
To dance for me

IF YOU CANNOT FIND HER

Tonight, the glow of the Moon
Bounces off the slick wet roads
It is otherwise dark
But it makes no difference

Because I am only alive in the night
The world is asleep
And silence makes its way into deep valleys
I am grateful for the silence
As it calms my chaotic mind

I do not deserve to witness this magic
But here I see like it is the first time
I've opened my dark brown eyes
I breathe it in and smile

Tomorrow this smile will disappear
So, I cup my hands to my chest
And pray tomorrow is a little late

If I am known for anything
I hope it is for LOVE

Please let it be LOVE

If the world is weight
Then that is what I shall carry

The weight of the world

SHEE

If all that I have written
    Is evidence of a broken heart
    Then I shall enlighten you

In between these thighs
    The ones that rub together
    The ones I am too insecure
    To let the Sun see

In between these two thighs
    You will find the ruins of war
    One I didn't win
    But one I was never supposed to fight

I survived

Fooling Who?

I tie my hair tighter than usual, to elongate my eyes. They are dark brown, and almond-like, accentuated with a liner, winged just to my liking. The eyeliner dark, pointy at the ends, symbolizing the two daggers I'm not brave enough to carry as protection from cat-callers who may become too touchy. To hold the daggers back, a pricey pair of faux lashes to make up for the lack of length in my own. My lips, deep red, almost the color of blood as it kisses oxygen for the first time, as it surfaces from a fresh wound. Two layers of the rouge, not one, because it lasts longer and I don't like to carry makeup in my bag, and I won't need reapplying. I look in the mirror, a heavy sigh follows. It was a mistake. I wipe it off. Who am I fooling anyway? There's not enough makeup in the world that can hide this broken.

I am not afraid of what this heart can do
But afraid of what it will allow

IF YOU CANNOT FIND HER

I've always made depression home
Small trips away
Yet I yearn for home
Scared to be gone too long
Separation anxiety

I want to move
Yet, I cannot find the strength
I am easily lost
But always find my way home

And if I could go back in time
I would have never looked you in the eyes
I would slip into the shadows
And admire you from afar
Because as much as I have loved you
The pain I have felt is more

IF YOU CANNOT FIND HER

I have a secret
One I'm too ashamed to share
Even if you don't deserve
To share this life with me

There are spaces in this heart
In which I leave vacant just for you
The days where I am weak
And all too forgiving

I light a floral path for you
So maybe
If you feel you need me
You can find your way
And rest your head upon the soft spots
That haven't yet hardened to stone

You don't deserve the soft spots
But I save them just for you

When I was broken
And didn't know it
I called myself *misunderstood*
Now, very much aware
I call myself a **_Poet_**

AWAKENING

IF YOU CANNOT FIND HER

All the years I abused it
When I took too much
And appreciated too little

Now as I age
I appreciate it as much as
A secret stash of fine wine
A limited supply
Left for me to achingly enjoy

All the while knowing someday
Nothing as sweet
Will ever touch my lips again

Time

SHEE

When you think of me
I hope it feels
Like a whisper in a dark room
An icy chill
That crawls up your spine
A scare that scars you
Long after your first encounter

I hope you realize
That I'm no longer waiting
No longer on your time
But I will continue to haunt you
Even from afar

IF YOU CANNOT FIND HER

I am always last
Always
I don't find this unfair
But instead an advantage

I watch everyone stumble
I watch them fall
I see their tears that stream
To fill the rivers and oceans

I see them drowning
Just by breathing air
I see them fight each other
To be victors of unworthy causes

I see everything
Only because I don't mind being last
I see everything
Because they do not feel as though
I am worthy to walk
Alongside them in their journeys

These are the lessons
And I am the student

So, I walk alone
And in my place

Because I am always last
Always

The Dark Side of the Moon

I loved you
I loved you before I knew what love was
I still love you
I love you because like me, you have a dark side
A dark side you could never share with the world

Would you share it even if you could?
Or do you covet your secrets like I covet you?
A dark side you wish wasn't so dark?
A dark side you wish you weren't ashamed of?

Like me, you have to hide the dark parts
Because those are not the parts we are supposed to have
Those are not the parts we are supposed to be proud of

They ignore their dark sides to make them feel superior
But we know that dark doesn't mean evil
We know dark doesn't mean bad
Dark means we appreciate the light even more than others

Dark means we are good at hiding
Dark means it hurts a little longer
Dark means we aren't afraid of being alone

Don't be ashamed of the dark
Because I love you and all of your darkness

IF YOU CANNOT FIND HER

When no one is looking
She dances with honeybees
In the lavender fields
Never has she felt so alive

For Fiona

SHEE

You gave up on me
Before I even took my first breath
Like it was the only choice you had

Not even a desire
To love me from afar
Because I know if you had
I would have felt it

I would have sensed
The gravitational pull
That the effect of love has
Even when not reciprocated
Or uncertain

You have always done your best
To be the negative to my positive
Forcing us further and further apart
Until there is nothing but nothing
Between who God destined us to be

Strangers

IF YOU CANNOT FIND HER

You're a book I crave to read
But will never finish
Because I am great at guessing endings
And I know how our story will end

I don't want us to end

Blame

All I've ever done is blame you
Blame you for my broken heart
The stunt in my emotional growth
The apparent frown upon my face

I told myself these were the side effects
Of searching for forgiveness
Trying my best to forgive you
For the things I had no answers for

But your journey is not mine
I am only a piece of your saturated thousand-piece puzzle
Only one piece

The forgiveness I have been looking for
Is the one I give myself
No more blame

I'm letting you go,
Because it is not fair for me to hold you hostage
Not when you are not done piecing yourself together

IF YOU CANNOT FIND HER

I attempted to write yesterday
But I found the words would not flow
They hid behind my skin like a child
Full of reluctance on her first day of school

The more I forced the pen
To brush paper
The words hid
They hid using the swollen
Sleep-deprived bags under my eyes as cover

They weren't ready to be written
So I closed my notebook
And gave them the day off
Hoping tomorrow they would be
Brave enough to be

Tomorrow will be yesterday soon enough

IF YOU CANNOT FIND HER

Does it upset you?
Does it make you mad?
That I do not name you once
Yet, you know it is you
I write most about

I won't say your name
Because that is giving you
More power in my life
Than you will ever deserve

Of all the things
That have broken me
I think you are
My favorite

How does love happen?

Breathe for me, she whispered.

Confused, he let out a breath.

Just like that, she smiled.

I write letters I know you'll never read.

Guilty pleasure

IF YOU CANNOT FIND HER

It is Spring
    And I am jealous of the flowers
    That are alive
    Because of Winter showers

It is Spring
    And all the Sun does
    Is want to give
    But here I hide
    Afraid to live

It is Spring
    And I am still me
    Afraid to bloom
    Afraid to be

SHEE

You don't believe in magic?
She questioned, disappointedly.

No! Magic is for fools!
You mean to tell me you do?
He giggled.

Yes, we all have magic...
She whispered.

Okay, Houdini, show me your magic!
He snickered.

So, she smiled and made him a believer.

Her magic was disguised as a smile.

IF YOU CANNOT FIND HER

I'm in love with
The way your footsteps
Kiss the pavement
Even if they are
To leave me behind

Here's the thing about falling (in love)
Most times, you don't know you've done it
Until you've already fallen

And,
> I had given you so much of me
> It was only in you
> Where I saw glimpses
> Of who I used to be

And,
> I hated you for accepting it all
> Knowing I would never say no
> To feel needed
> Was my kryptonite

And,
> Now she will never be mine
> That girl who needed
> But gave it all instead

And,
> Maybe that was my purpose
> I'm all used up
> There is no more
> No more to give

I swallow my cry
And it feels as though
Shards of glass glitter my throat
I won't allow you to see me cry
Ever.
Again.

No matter how much it hurts

Forgive them for their tragedies in love
Maybe they haven't had enough practice in caring for
something as fragile as a heart

———

Be gentle with yourself when it comes to mishaps in love
You just need a little practice

SHEE

She was always off
Fighting another person's war
Saving and sacrificing
It was her way
Fighting for anyone
And everyone she loved

But that's the thing
She was always battling for others
She could never fight her own
No one ever stepped up for her
Because they didn't think she needed the help

Help her
She needs the help

IF YOU CANNOT FIND HER

You're a love song I know by memory
A song full of decadent words
All the words are beautiful
All the words make me flutter with glee

Written thoughtfully
Like they are just for me
My favorite love song

We walked into the fire
A testament to our love
We were willing and brave
But only one of us walked out of there
The other enjoyed the flames

IF YOU CANNOT FIND HER

Today, it is in between the dark spaces
Of heavy sighs and silent screams
Where you will find the pain
It is always there
Always

SHEE

Some children wish
To give their mothers the world
Not me

Not for lack of ambition
Or a lack to fulfill desires

Mama, if I could give you anything
It would be the Moon
Because if we were to ever find ourselves apart
The glow of the Moon
Will lead me back to you

Mahal Kita, Inay

IF YOU CANNOT FIND HER

The flow of his name
Through the split of her lips
Was not a prophecy
But a deep-seated wish

SHEE

See, we are all born with wings
But we are only given the power to use them
When it is our time to fly

Rest in Love Emilio V.

The long way home
Wasn't long enough
So we traveled a path
Unfamiliar to us both
And called it *Love*

The road was rocky
At times, we tripped and fell
The journey rough
Tears constant
Racing down our face

Obstacle after obstacle
We were often lost
Losing trust in
Each other's sense of direction
Losing confidence in our decision

To walk an unknown path
But we kept going
And, there were good times
Laughter
Romance
And even peace

It was anything but easy
But it was ours
Love was ours

SHEE

I grew up wishing my eyes were blue
Now, as I'm older
I love the secrecy of these dark brown eyes
I don't think I'd care much to walk around
With eyes that predict my whole life

Blue

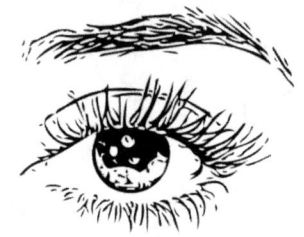

IF YOU CANNOT FIND HER

I lift the forgotten plant
Stare at its limp leaves
And wilting flowers

How could I have forgotten
To take care of something so fragile?

I pluck the withered leaves
And whisper my apologies

I hydrate it with fresh water
And let it bathe in the Sun

I guess we all forget about the things we love
Even if unintentional

For you, it was me
I'm not a plant
But delicate still

You do not try to bring me back
From my diminished state
You leave me in dirt
That was once fertile soil

I'm here hoping
Someone will come around one day
To bring me back to life

Hoping someone
Someday
Will want me

I'm tired of missing a person
I'm not certain you ever were

IF YOU CANNOT FIND HER

You use my history as ammunition
For an imaginary gun you hold to my head
You might as well shoot me in the chest
Because it is my heart that remembers pain
My brain is just full of regrets

And, for some reason
I've always given up on myself

But never on you

Autumn

It is Autumn and the leaves have started to fall
They fall with such grace
That it reminds me falling isn't so bad

I take my hands out of my pockets
Exposing them to the chilly Autumn evening
And I grab hold of a dancing leaf
That is making its way down
To commune with the Earth

I hold it to my heart
Like I am trying to bring it back to life
With the rhythm within my chest

Autumn is your most beloved season
And we are not together to see it unfold

So, I whisper your name on to the leaf
And set it down gently onto the soil

Spring will come soon enough
And new life will come from that very leaf
And that will somehow be enough
Even if we never were

Until Autumn comes again

Why poetry?
They ask…

Drugs are too expensive

IF YOU CANNOT FIND HER

Darling, that one is going to take a lifetime to heal.
    -Your Heart

The color of a traumatic history
Fuck colonization
The color I was taught to loathe as a child
Anak, don't go in the Sun you'll get <u>too</u> dark

The color of strength and courage
The color of culture and roots
The color of purpose and worth
The color of devotion and perseverance

The color I embrace as a mother
The color I romance as a woman
The color I defend as a person
The color I fight for as a human

This color I am
This color we are
Brown

What I never did

I'm sorry for that too

Maybe it's the Moon's fault
Why I only fall in love at night

Maybe

You made me believe that these petals (soft and free of imperfection) were what attracted your love — the innocence, these fragile, never-been touched gifts of silk. Little did I know it was my seeds (fruitful and full of potential) you were after. You told me you would keep them safe and out of harm's way. Never believe what you cannot see because before I realized I wanted them back, you had hidden them in a pit of darkness (all you wanted was something to control). I realized too late that these petals are only beauty and those seeds my way towards growth.

Don't lose yourself in a person who has no idea how to help a flower grow.

If you feel like you're missing something
I'm sorry
I knew I was losing you
So, I took a few pieces of you
And, hid them in the folds of my heart
Don't bother getting them back
Because this heart is a labyrinth
I have yet to find my way out

IF YOU CANNOT FIND HER

Maybe her love wasn't meant for you
Because even though a flower blooms for the Sun
Who is to say she doesn't stay awake for the Moon

Oh, the tragedies we call love.

IF YOU CANNOT FIND HER

You wanted sometimes
And…
I was only capable of forever

SHEE

Maybe one day
We can meet for brunch
And we can share stories
About who we are as people

About who we grew to be
Laugh and giggle
As we spill out funny memories
Listen with patience
As we spew out pieces of pain

Maybe one day
I can stop pretending
That we will be reunited
That there will ever be a chance
To look past the divide

No matter how hurt
How broken
This heart is ever the optimist

IF YOU CANNOT FIND HER

One day I am strong and brave
The next, weak and timid
One day I am in love with love
The next, cursing this foolish heart

One day I appreciate the lessons
The next, I wallow in the pain of my past
I am in a constant state of contradiction
And, there is not much I can do to help it

The taste of your name is always bitter…

―――――――――――――――――――――――――――――
Name Here

IF YOU CANNOT FIND HER

Your first mistake was believing
They could ever love you
The way you loved them
The second,
Believing it did not matter
When you realized they could not

One-sided love

SHEE

Please tell me
If there is no room
In your life for me
Instead of opening the door
Enough for me to see hope
But not nearly enough
For me to touch it

When I say
I am not the one
It is because once
I was the one who wrestled demons
While everyone watched me struggle

I was the one who cried whole oceans
While holding up mountains
So others wouldn't drown
I was the one who came back
From the edge of a crumbling cliff
To find solid ground for others to walk on

So, when I say
I am not the one
Believe me
I will no longer put myself
In situations that rip me to pieces
While others stay whole

SHEE

> He wanted a love song
> But she would only ever be
> An unfinished POEM

Happiness lurks behind closed doors
Peeping through keyholes
And under locked doors
To see if it is her time

I ignore her
I am not ready to grasp her hand
Even though she is eager to hold mine

She waits patiently and longingly
In dark corners
I cannot help
But be distracted

By her shine
She smiles at me
But I look away
So beautiful it hurts to stare

I keep her near
But not too close
Temptation always healthier
Kept at a safe distance away

Unrequited Happiness

If love were a battlefield,

Baby, we lost the war

IF YOU CANNOT FIND HER

I traveled my life through back roads
And forgotten trails
More times alone
Then I would care to share

I've held hands with ghosts
And shadows
Who left me time
And time again

I will never take the light for granted
After darkness spoke my name
Darkness is nor friend, nor foe
No enemy of mine

But I am grateful for its presence daily
As I am who it has built

SHEE

I don't do easy
Look at the disaster that is my past
The evidence all there
I continue to do things the hard way
But if my history has taught me anything
It is, easy does not build resilience
Easy does not give you tough skin
Easy does not make you smarter
And it certainly doesn't
Make you love harder

I wanted to be your rock
But even rocks crumble with time

The Sands of Time

Darling, it was meant to hurt.
 -Your Heart

IF YOU CANNOT FIND HER

The reasons I found you
Are the same reasons I lost me

SHEE

The signs you need me:
>   The unfolded laundry that sits piled in baskets
>   The wrinkled bed sheets on our unmade bed
>   The piling dishes in the messy kitchen
>   The leaking faucet in the upstairs bathroom

The evidence you don't want me:
>   The unwritten love letters sprayed with your scent
>   The kiss-less mornings I sit alone drinking coffee
>   The dinners alone, where I cook your favorite meals
>   The broken promises, you said you'd never break

The signs are everywhere of how much you need me.

The evidence, nowhere, of how much you want me.

IF YOU CANNOT FIND HER

Sometimes, all we need is a hug
      Not to fix us
    But to hold us together

SHEE

She is wild with fantasy
Dreams and intimacy
Yet, she does not know
She is not dreaming
Yet, she is not awake

Only when she is free
Will she touch what is not visible to most
It must be her who stumbles
Across her journey
Without direction from those
With unclear intentions

Let her be wild
Let her be free
Let her BE

IF YOU CANNOT FIND HER

And I blame my heart
For bullying my brain
For manipulating strength
Into weakness

And making me believe
I deserve less
Then what I want

And for what it is worth
I blame my brain
For believing my heart

Sometimes we tell ourselves that
What we are missing is closure
Like the closure will sew up our wounds
And they will never be tender again
Don't be mistaken

Closure hurts too

IF YOU CANNOT FIND HER

I wish I could rescue myself
From the days I drowned
In the thought of you
But who am I kidding?
Everyone knows
I'm not a strong swimmer

Anymore
Last night I dreamt you loved me
But to remember is a force never dormant for too long
Woken by salty tears and a revelation
That dreams are sometimes lies dressed in hopes

I realized no amount of love
Could make up for the amount of pain you've caused
Last night I dreamt you loved me
But I don't want that anymore

Anak, be proud of your baby hairs and melanin.

Nagagalak na ako

We do not cherish the ugly
We let it sit in the back
With a lack of appreciation

We dismiss it
Like it hasn't given us courage
Like it hasn't given us strength

Maybe if we held its hand
And said, *thank you*
We would see it
For what it truly is

Beauty

IF YOU CANNOT FIND HER

And I'm terrible in arguments
The words erupt
But they come out weak
And insecure

The only way I can defend myself
Is through my poetry
And always out of the argument

What does it matter?
We know you don't read my poems

Yet, I keep writing
Hoping someday
I'll be heard

SHEE

Of all the things
I have ever loved
It was not me
Whom, I loved enough

IF YOU CANNOT FIND HER

Peace beckons me
But I trip
Before it is mine

SHEE

Depression decided to stop by unannounced today
Now, as he overstays his welcome
I do my best to get away
But he likes my company too much
And, although I am exhausted
I cannot bear to hurt his feelings
So, I let him stay

An Expected Visitor

IF YOU CANNOT FIND HER

I don't have the heart to tell the ocean
I swim in her waters
And walk her lonely shores
Just to feel the pull of the Moon

Or to tell the meadows
I run through her blooming butterfly-filled fields
Always as the sunsets
So I can welcome the Moon with song and dance

I'm not brave enough
To reveal to the mountains
That I only use its strength-filled forms
And its highest peaks as stepping stones

To be closer to the Moon
Knowing I'll never touch him
The way he's touched me
Knowing I am only a human

A human who wishes to be the sky
Because it is the sky who cradles the Moon
And, what I'd do for a chance to show the Moon
How much he is loved

And here I am fighting
Fighting to be remembered
In a world that is so forgetful
Don't forget me

IF YOU CANNOT FIND HER

If it is not within you to love me
I won't beg
Because even in a world
Where the Sun misses the Moon
It does not stop it from rising

SHEE

I've driven myself crazy
Questioning if you think of me
Wondering if it hurts
Knowing how much you missed out on
And then there are days
I know the answer
And the answer is
I'm the only one who hurts

There is a universe where scars are revered like the galaxies
Where we speak our truth and don't cave into fallacies
Where boundaries like no and stop are respected
And beauty is what beauty is and never is perfected

See, in this universe I would have a Daddy
One who stayed and one who loved me
My pedophile would have been a bibliophile
Who taught me how to read
Instead of how to hate
What God gave me in between my knees

And, maybe I come up with these ideas
bBecause I'm too ashamed to face
That much of what I have been through you call disgrace
Or perhaps I'm a believer that good will always win
Even if we carry the weight of others
Who are evil and commit sin

Those who have a problem with your story
Are usually the ones who gave you a story to write

When love is the problem
  It is also the solution

SHEE

Love was like a lonely journey
Towards finding a place called home
Bravery pushed out of me
Enough to make me move
On that doubt-filled road
I found another lonely soul
I found you
I claimed you

The place I call my HOME

IF YOU CANNOT FIND HER

And when I met you
I knew I'd suffocate because
I wouldn't allow myself to exhale
In fear of losing you
So, I lost myself instead
And you never cared to find me

I won't give you
The satisfaction of believing
You were the one to break my heart
It was broken long before you ever met me
Jokes on you

IF YOU CANNOT FIND HER

I can always tell the night I will have
By the color of the sky when the Sun sets
Tonight, it is amber
The color of your skin
I can always tell the night I will have
When the Sun sets
Tonight, I will cry

I didn't mean to be war
I tried to be the peace you wanted
But how did you expect me
To sit and choose silence
When you fought against me
Not for me

Like the plucking of a rose
So beautiful and plump
But as quick as we pick
We are quicker to toss

No longer beautiful
But wilted
And brittle instead

I no longer pick roses
I admire them
From the stem

SHEE

If I woke one day
And this was all a dream
I would fall back to sleep
To find my way back to you

You hand it to me
Like it is meant to be mine
Like I do not own enough of it
Yet I welcome it with open arms
Because if that is the only
Piece of you
You are willing to share
I'll take it
And cherish it
For what it is

Pain

Tonight, I will cry to the Moon
When the world is asleep in their beds
I'll whisper my heartbreak into the night
And bathe in the glow of the stars

IF YOU CANNOT FIND HER

How did we get here?
   This missing who we never were...

SHEE

Sip warm tea with Heartbreak
And listen to her woes
Give her love
Kiss her wounds
And tuck her in for the night
Take her on picnics
And long walks in the park
Hold her hand towards healing
And she will be all right

She's the type of girl
To serenade the Moon
Moon Lover

SHEE

Forgotten flowers bloom
Although, you'd never know
They bloom only when
The Moon decorates the night
And when the world has gone to sleep
They dance in silver Moonlight
And cry blue salted tears
Forgotten flowers bloom

I. Still. Bloom

IF YOU CANNOT FIND HER

Your smile
Like warm honey
I just want a taste

Sometimes we do not stand
For what we believe in
Sometimes, we march
Sometimes, we sit
And, sometimes
Sometimes, we kneel

Twisted Wishes

Is it a surprise that I desire
To break free from our twisted ceremonies
Where we scream
Where I cry
Where you fuck me (over)
Where we come face to face
And almost say goodbye

But neither of us are immune to the force
That keeps us entangled in a rotting dependency
And I can't help but think of the adolescent teenage girl
Eager for love (daddy issues)
The one who prayed to falling stars
And who wrote angst filled wishes under her sleeves

Because in fact, I got love
Love wrapped in thorns
But love, nonetheless
Which is undeniable evidence
That the universe has a twisted sense of humor
And don't for one minute believe if it is granted
That wish is free

Don't wish for anything you're not brave enough to fight for

Now hush as I make this wish
Please let us make it

SHEE

I try so hard not to care
About being left behind
But I still wait
Anxiously
I wait because maybe
You'll realize it was a mistake
And that I'm worth it after all

The force that pushes us together
Is the same force that pulls us apart
The determining factor
Of this push and pull?

You

Me

Us

Some days you'll have to pretend
That the Sun rises just for you
To survive the darkest nights
Honey, it will rise
Honey rise

IF YOU CANNOT FIND HER

I've bled under sweaters
By sharp nails washed clean
No evidence to the outside world
Not that they'd even lose sleep

I've mourned losses of those who still breathe
Those who forget I exist
Those I love and need

I've laughed through tears
To escape thoughts of death
Yet, this heart loves and is kind
Even if this world is not

SHEE

The thing with selfish people is
They don't care if they're selfish
They'll take
And take
Even if they have more than enough

The thing with givers is
They don't care too much
If those they love
Don't care for them
They'll give
And give
Even if they have
Nothing left for themselves
Even love

IF YOU CANNOT FIND HER

You may wonder if I feel sorry for myself
If I sit and wallow in self-pity
Don't
Because even if I feel sorry for the person I was
I am damn proud of the person I've become

SHEE

You've taken more from me than
I have ever received from you
Yet, it is never enough

I've done my best for years
To leave you behind
But you always manage to catch up

One day I hope I will be free from you
Although, I'm sure it wouldn't last

So, instead of losing precious time
Figuring out how to rid you from my future
I will allow us to coexist in the now

IF YOU CANNOT FIND HER

I loved you before I ever loved myself
Expecting you to teach me how
It was only in the ways
You did not love me
Where I learned I could
Love me all on my own

Trust Issues

You say I have trust issues
And I won't deny it
If not an open book
I am an accessible poem for all to read
So, I admit—Hell yes!
I have issues with trust
Because the same people
Who were meant to protect me
Looked the other way when I was violated as a child

Because the pills that were intended to take away pain
Weren't even strong enough to take away mine
Because the same man who helped give me life
Could care less if I existed in his
Because the people who say they support me
Can't even tell you why I write

I realize no one owes me anything
Nothing is rightfully mine
Not even these words
So I trust nothing
Not even the Moon
Because even the Moon has no choice but to say goodbye

When you sit alone, thinking you're doing life wrong, what you're really doing is thinking about life wrong. This life is about trial and error, lessons being learned, and rising above things that are out of our control. There is no guidebook; no roadmap with an X. We stress ourselves out, searching for explanations from people who have no intentions of seeing us succeed. No one should want more for you than you should want for yourself. Stop. Stop thinking life will somehow reveal its secret message to you. The secret is, you are amazing. Look how damn far you've come. Look at what you've overcome. You've walked a million miles in a body you may hate. You've seen a billion stars through eyes you pretend are blind. You've created and crafted with beautiful hands that you use to close doors of opportunity. You have loved so deep with a heart you allow others to break. Stop. Promise me, wait, no… Promise your damn self you will look yourself in the mirror and tell yourself how, even if you do not love yourself today, you will do your best tomorrow to find your way towards loving YOU in ways no other person on this Earth can do. Only you can stop thinking wrong about life. Only you. Only you can cherish what little time you have left on this lonely planet. So, make it worth it, and want for yourself what you wish for others you love.

SHEE

Can you not give me
These things that make me, me?
Why must you take and take
Until I am in the shadows
Of what used to resemble joy

These bits and pieces
I worked so hard to find
Only for you to pick at me
Like you own these fragments
As if you've created them on your own

How could you take credit for my hard work?
Without knowing what I've endured
How could I have forgotten
That shallow people
With selfish tendencies
Have the prettiest smiles

Plagiarism

IF YOU CANNOT FIND HER

I wanted forever
Now, I'd take one day

There were moments
When I wouldn't allow myself to breathe
Unless I held you in my arms
Now, breathing only comes
When you're gone

And, I cradled time
Hoping it would change our fate
Wishing it would mend old wounds
Praying it would erase the broken
But I learned miserably
You can never hold onto time
You can only let it go

I choose to live in the past most days
Silly?
Maybe

But, don't be fooled
I'm broken there too

IF YOU CANNOT FIND HER

I know you owe me nothing
Because simply
That is what you've made of me

But if your heart is willing
Please one request
Two minutes
Just two

So, if I never see you again
I'll give you one last kiss
And tell you how I love you
And that'll be our end

SHEE

See, the thing is
If you listen closely
You can hear the damage in her voice
So, she sings
Hoping to disguise the frailty as sweet melody
Does it work?
Can you hear it in song?
The broken?

IF YOU CANNOT FIND HER

And, nowhere in your life
Is there evidence that I ever existed
That I was ever a part of your journey
You cut me out like a cancer
Something unwanted
Yet something, just trying to survive

SHEE

The truth is
I only share in halves

Not intentionally, really
But that is all anyone allows from me

And yet even though I want
The ones I love in wholes

They're not even capable
Of giving me half

IF YOU CANNOT FIND HER

Sometimes God gives us gifts
That we take for granted
Is that what happened?
If so, tell me
And, I will make my way
Towards understanding

If this heart
Within this chest of mine
Has me broken
Does that mean I am but
A fracture within the universe
Sweetie, we are how the lights get in…

IF YOU CANNOT FIND HER

The fact that you had to quit me in the first place
Helps ease the pain of knowing
You let go so easily
For, once upon a time
You loved me
And, maybe that is enough
BTW, you suck at forever

Beginnings are just endings with a chance

IF YOU CANNOT FIND HER

Sunsets are promises to the Moon
Because even the Sun knows
Everyone deserves a chance to shine

Love…
It
Is
The
Only
Way

IF YOU CANNOT FIND HER

Your intentions were like bricks upon my chest
And a blindfold upon my eyes
Blinded by hope
Suffocated by optimism
I let you break me
Because what good is a story
Without a bit of heartbreak

SHEE

If you've only ever had yourself
Then maybe that's all you've ever needed

IF YOU CANNOT FIND HER

If writing were a sin
I'd take you to hell with me
My muse

SHEE

I have lost my mind on many occasions
But it has always been my heart
That has driven me crazy

IF YOU CANNOT FIND HER

      I am a forgotten
    A child of bitter consequences
   A product of a loveless mix up
      A question of worth
       A count of tears
       A learned lesson

      I am a forgotten

They tell you to go where the love is
But what if you are love?

Baby, just be...

IF YOU CANNOT FIND HER

You warned me loving you
Would only kill me
Here I am
Loving you from the grave

All things end
Even endings

IF YOU CANNOT FIND HER

I am in a constant state of finding myself
Hide and seek

SHEE

Prayer is the only thing
    I can think of
    To keep my hold of you
    Because we all know
    Wishes are not sacred enough

So, I close my eyes to you
    And fall fast into prayer
    I am incapacitated
    From the weight of the world
    And the chaos that is my life

But you,
    You are grace in a world of fire
    You are clarity in this distorted mess
    Of all the things I continue to hold
    It is only you who gives me hope
    For a better tomorrow

Some days she cried herself to tomorrow
She wept full oceans, alone
She survived storms, that were her own
And, some days
She cried herself to tomorrow
Darling, if that's what it takes
Cry

He was the first to call her beautiful

You know the broken girls always fall for that

IF YOU CANNOT FIND HER

We were young
Living for the days
We could escape to dance
In the mustard flower fields
Behind our broken home

Our clothes stained yellow
From rolling around
Those innocent blooms

Now, every time I see
Those lovely yellow petals
It brings me back
To when unassuming little flowers
Had the power to keep us from falling
When everything else in our lives was crumbling

I'm sure they didn't mind holding us up
Even if it was only
A few millimeters off the ground
Embracing our rowdy
So we didn't hit the dirt

Even If that's where
Life said we belonged

Amy, Josie, Joann, & Joseph

SHEE

Remember when we craved the wild?
How we would slip away
And run like we were running towards freedom?
How sunsets were our queues
To release us from our chains
Remember when we were in love in the wild?
What happened to our love?
Did it get lost in the wild?

IF YOU CANNOT FIND HER

There are infinite, infinities
Within our silence
And I am living each one
Over and over
The pain goes on

SHEE

Last night
I sat alone
Watching cotton candy clouds
Dance across the sky

I didn't want to blink
I didn't want to breathe
I was afraid the subtle force
Of the blink and the breath

Would only make
That moment fade faster
And, for a second
That moment was mine

For a second
I held that moment in my heart
And then it was gone
Gone with a blink of an eye
And a release of a breath

I wonder if that is what death feels like
I wonder if it is beautiful
Beautiful and yours

IF YOU CANNOT FIND HER

Wear your broken like a smile

I will wrap these wounds with love
Mend this heart with understanding
Embrace these scars with forgiveness
Nurture this soul with goodness
I promise

Promises to my future self...

IF YOU CANNOT FIND HER

The first man a girl loves
Should be the man
Who will help her
Mend her first broken heart
Instead, the first man she ever loved
Was also the first man
To break her heart

SHEE

I loved your dark parts the most
I yearn for them still
I hold onto them
These bits and pieces of darkness
Swimming around our story

I loved them
Even though those are the parts
That broke me to pieces

Why?
Because no one else saw those parts
Those are the parts you only shared with me
Everyone loves a good secret

And that was ours

IF YOU CANNOT FIND HER

Everything this skin has felt
 This heart has felt it first

SHEE

If innocence could talk
It would never whisper
It would scream its lungs bloody
Because no one ever listens
It would fight like a lion
Protecting its young
But it won't be enough
It is never enough
Innocence lost
Won't find its way home

IF YOU CANNOT FIND HER

Nothing is ever gone, is it?
I still hear our love
Howling in the wind

The words come to me
Like the waves upon the shore

Build up
Release
Build up
Release

This damage we've caused
This line we've crossed
This ignorance we've shown

What is this?
This mess we've made
This man you are
This woman I've become
This

What is this?
This isn't you
This isn't me
This isn't US

SHEE

I was lonely today
But I danced in the rain anyway
All these universes
In the form of droplets
Danced upon my skin
As I danced upon the Earth
I was lonely today
But I danced
Baby, I danced

IF YOU CANNOT FIND HER

He kept trying to be the Sun
When all she needed was the Moon

SHEE

>She fell in love with Tomorrow
>But Tomorrow always changed its name
>So, she took it as it was
>And fell in love with Today

IF YOU CANNOT FIND HER

The passing of time
Tones down our words

To soft whispers
Breathy words

The words are faint
Soft and subtle

Yet, I hear them
I still hear us

Here…
Hear us

SHEE

And we fell in slow motion
All the while
Looking into each other's eyes
Wrapped in happiness
Immune to the world
But here we are
Now with two hearts
Tender and bruised
Trying to find the lucky stones
That made us first fall

IF YOU CANNOT FIND HER

I don't remember
I said
But I remembered
I always remember
But, saying it out loud
Was like proof of our failure
To remain how we once were

SHEE

Both no strangers to addiction
Intense disease
Fierce affliction
You, always high
Me, always low
Bound tight together
We can't let go
Addicted to drugs
Addicted to love
What will you choose?
When push comes to shove

IF YOU CANNOT FIND HER

I hate to admit it
But I let myself go
I allowed this brittle heart
Of mine to succumb
To the darkness the world
Calls depression

The darkness crept itself
Into every crevice it could find
Suffocating the light
Away from my heart
Twisting my soul into
Something unfamiliar

We speak of bullies
Who walk amongst us
Spewing venom
In the form of words
But those are the bullies
We need not be afraid of

The biggest bully
I've ever encountered
Is sadly
Myself

SHEE

She fell in wonder
Unable to attach herself to reality

She fell because
No one could offer her
Anything but a fall

What will you offer her?
Let her fall
Let her wonder
Let her dream

But give her something
She doesn't need
To sleep away

Let it be love
Please
Let it be love

IF YOU CANNOT FIND HER

And in my future
Despite my trials
I will remember
To be kind to myself
To allow myself to heal
To love myself harder
Even when I feel
Like giving up
To forgive myself for failing
And I will remind myself
That I am human
Of flesh and bone
I will exist and feel
On my own terms

SHEE

These words are fluid
They float in time
Symbols of the past
And present
And of future desires
These fluid words
Are symbols of a life
A life called, Mine

IF YOU CANNOT FIND HER

Inside
Inside this love
You will find danger
You will find sanctuary
Inside
Inside this love
You will find thorns
You will find roses
Inside
Inside this love
You will find rage
You will find peace
Inside
Inside this love
You will find me
You will find me

SHEE

You've never had to question my love
I loved hard
Hard enough for the both of us

There was never a day
Where I made you work for something
You promised to reciprocate

But here I am ready to leave
Still worried about keeping you together
Still worried about keeping you whole

IF YOU CANNOT FIND HER

Once upon a time
I wrote poems on my skin
Words
Sad words
Only I could understand
Hidden under sweaters
And long sleeves
Nothing I was ever
Brave enough to share
Stronger now
I write my weaknesses
With my pen

I have walked my journey
On a fractured path
The path is mine
It is mine
All the cracks are mine

IF YOU CANNOT FIND HER

We pick at our wounds
Because we aren't ready
To let them heal
We look for ways
To hold onto what
Hurt us in the first place
Because we have been led
To believe that is what we deserve
No Dear…
Let the wound heal

We look for people
To set our hearts on fire
Darling, we are fire!
We were all born flames

IF YOU CANNOT FIND HER

I jumped heart first
Into the ocean I claimed for us
But I drowned
Because even if you love something
It doesn't mean it's yours

SHEE

To my body
Please forgive me
For the days I purged
Because I felt you were
Too full at the seams
And for the days I cut myself
To make the mental pain
Go away
And for the time I tried
To take my life
Because I didn't know love
I know you have walked
A million miles
Recovered from my destruction
And bore four beautiful souls
And for that
I thank you
And even though
You owe me nothing
Please don't give up on me now

IF YOU CANNOT FIND HER

A long time ago
I demanded we meet
I showed up
Thinking I was ready to be yours
Instead you didn't show
You left me to deal
With what I felt I could not
LIFE
But I know you have a sense of humor
And one day
You will come knocking
When I want you the least
Regretting my desire
To ever meet you
Death

SHEE

I tried my best to resist your love
Because I knew once I melted
I'd never have the strength
To be whole again without you

IF YOU CANNOT FIND HER

> You don't get to hurt me
> And then
> Tell me how to heal

The greatest villain
In her journey
Was also
The love
Of her life

IF YOU CANNOT FIND HER

If you cannot find her
You will find her in words

Look, you've found me

acknowledgments

To everyone who helped to make this dream come true, thank you from the bottom of my heart. I love you all.

Special Thanks:
Andres (My Love)
My babies
My Mama
Amy K.
Uriel M.
Elizabeth M.
Kayla M.
Daniel C.
Marlette P.
Bianca R.
Chloe W.
Georgina M.
Selin S.
Lady Fiona
M. Tagramere

about the author

Shee is a Filipina American poet and writer, currently living in the Bay Area of California. Her interests include writing, reading, hiking, photography, traveling, and spending time with her husband and children. This is her first collection of poetry.

www.ingramcontent.com/pod-product-compliance
Lightning Source LLC
LaVergne TN
LVHW051516070426
835507LV00023B/3143